LES PETITS PLATS
FRANÇAIS
SIMON & SCHUSTER
ILLUSTRATED

fabulous fondant desserts

PAUL SIMON

Photography by Akiko Ida

Styling by Stéphanie Huré

SIMON &
SCHUSTER

London · New York · Sydney · Toronto

A CBS COMPANY

English language edition published in Great Britain by
Simon and Schuster UK Ltd, 2010
A CBS Company

Copyright © Marabout 2010

SIMON AND SCHUSTER ILLUSTRATED BOOKS
Simon & Schuster UK
222 Gray's Inn Road
London WC1X 8HB
www.simonandschuster.co.uk

1 2 3 4 5 6 7 8 9 10

Styling for photography: Stéphanie Huré

Translation: Prudence Ivey
Copy editor English language: Nicki Lampon

Colour reproduction by Dot Gradations Ltd, UK
Printed and bound in U.A.E.

ISBN 978-0-85720-108-9

Contents

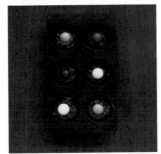

Equipment

For the fondants

Silicone moulds: Round, square and heart-shaped, these are all useful for making individual fondant puddings. All you need to do is line the bottom with a circle of greaseproof paper and put on a baking tray (also covered with greaseproof paper). Turn out with a metal spatula and peel off the paper. If you follow these instructions, they should turn out perfectly!

Metal moulds and paper cases: These are also very useful. Metal moulds that have been greased and dusted with flour are very easy to manipulate; paper cases look pretty and allow you to turn the puddings out really quickly – they are ideal for picnics.

Silicone mould trays: You can find these in all shapes and sizes. They are not always ideal for making fondant puddings as they can be more difficult to manipulate. For really runny-centred puddings, trays can make turning out arduous. Consider covering the bottom of the moulds with greaseproof paper so as not to lose a single crumb.

For the centres

A tray of small hemispherical moulds will be your best friend when making the little ganache centres (see page 28). You can, however, use an ice cube tray.

Ready in 15 minutes...

All these recipes are easy to make; they need only a little preparation time, sometimes a little resting time. They surprise, they reassure, they fill, they ooze...

Only 15 minutes is needed to satisfy your sweet tooth with a good fondant dessert – as attractive as a goose down pillow on an evening when you're really tired.

Only 15 minutes to feel the chocolate or caramel melt in your mouth and be enveloped by an intense pleasure – a pure moment of gluttony.

Attention, handle with care!
Cooking fondant-centred puddings is a delicate art, like all baking. Oven temperatures are not always reliable and can vary considerably depending on the model of oven or whether it is fan-assisted, gas or electric.

Most of the recipes in the book have been tested using moulds 7 cm (2¾ inches) in diameter and 4.5 cm (1¾ inches) tall; the size of the moulds or cases can affect the cooking time considerably and change the texture of the cakes. This is why it is always necessary to check the cooking.

Customise your fondants
The following basic recipes will suffice to satisfy any sweet tooth. But there is also a panoply of confectionery that you can experiment with.

Don't hesitate to raid the shops for chocolate bars, sweets, sweet spreads, jams and other chocolates, pralines and sweet things.

If you slip in a morsel of one, or a few teaspoons of the other, you'll transform your fondant into a veritable surprise dessert. Maximum effect for minimum effort...

Let your imagination run wild: hundreds of combinations await you!

The essential dark chocolate fondant

Preparation time: 10 minutes
Cooking time: 6–7 minutes
Makes 4 fondants

2 eggs
50 g (1¾ oz) brown sugar
1 dessertspoon plain flour
1 dessertspoon cornflour
140 g (5 oz) dark chocolate
  (minimum 70% cocoa solids),
  broken into small pieces
110 g (4 oz) butter
3 dessertspoons whipping cream

Preheat the oven to 200°C (fan oven 180°C), Gas Mark 6.

Use four metal moulds. Grease and dust with flour or line with baking parchment. Place them on a baking tray covered with greaseproof paper.

Beat the eggs and sugar together until the mixture turns pale. Sieve the flour and cornflour together, add to the mixture and continue to beat.

Melt the chocolate, butter and cream in a bowl over a pan of simmering water.

Pour the chocolate cream into the sponge mixture and mix until you have a smooth paste.

Fill the moulds, put in the oven and cook for 6–7 minutes. The cakes should be very soft to the touch. Turn out of the moulds and serve straight away.

Tip: If you decide to fill the cakes with dark chocolate, jam or any other treat, it is important to leave the raw mix in the fridge for at least an hour before using so that it becomes denser.

Four variations on a dark chocolate fondant

Make the basic fondant mixture (see page 8).

Half fill the greased and floured moulds with the mixture then place one of the following on top…

Totally chocolate *(top left)*
2 squares of dark chocolate

Praline centre *(bottom left)*
1 square of pralinoise (French praline chocolate available online) or milk chocolate with peanuts

Caramel centre *(top right)*
1 teaspoon of caramel

Black cherry *(bottom right)*
1 teaspoon of black cherry jam

…now fill the moulds two-thirds of the way up with the remaining mixture and cook as on page 8.

Tip: If you're worried about turning the fondants out, leave to cool, turn out then re-heat them in the microwave before serving.

Milk chocolate fondants

Preparation time: 10 minutes
Cooking time: 6–7 minutes
Makes 4 fondants

3 eggs
80 g (2¾ oz) caster sugar
1 dessertspoon plain flour
150 g (5¼ oz) milk chocolate,
  broken into small pieces
40 g (1½ oz) butter

Preheat the oven to 200°C (fan oven 180°C), Gas Mark 6.

Use four metal moulds. Grease and dust with flour or line with baking parchment. Place them on a baking tray covered with greaseproof paper.

Beat the eggs and sugar together until pale. Sieve the flour, add to the mixture and continue to beat.

Melt the milk chocolate and butter in a bowl over a pan of simmering water.

Add the melted chocolate to the sponge mixture and mix to a smooth paste.

Fill the moulds with the mixture and cook for 6–7 minutes. The cakes should be very soft to the touch. Turn out and serve immediately.

Tip: The cooking time will determine how liquid the fondant will be.

Four variations on a milk chocolate fondant

Make the basic fondant mixture (see page 12).

Half fill the greased and floured moulds with the mixture then place one of the following on top…

Totally chocolate *(top left)*
2 squares of milk chocolate

Toffee centre *(bottom left)*
2 soft caramels, softened and rolled into a ball

Twix *(top right)*
½ a Twix bar, crushed and rolled into a ball

Nutella *(bottom right)*
1 teaspoon of Nutella

…**now** fill the moulds two-thirds of the way up with the remaining mixture and cook as on page 12.

Tip: These suggestions can be used in any of the basic chocolate fondant recipes.

White chocolate fondants

Preparation time: 10 minutes
Cooking time: 6–7 minutes
Makes 4 fondants

3 eggs
75 g (2½ oz) caster sugar
3 dessertspoons plain flour
1 dessertspoon ground almonds
130 g (4½ oz) white chocolate,
  broken into small pieces
60 g (2 oz) butter
2 dessertspoons whipping cream

Preheat the oven to 200°C (fan oven 180°C), Gas Mark 6.

Use four metal dessert moulds. Grease and dust with flour or line with baking parchment. Place them on a baking tray covered with greaseproof paper.

Beat the eggs and sugar together until pale. Sieve the flour and ground almonds together, add to the mixture and continue to beat.

Melt the chocolate, butter and cream in a bowl over a pan of simmering water (make sure the white chocolate does not get too hot).

Add the chocolate cream to the sponge mixture and mix to a smooth paste.

Fill the moulds two-thirds full and cook for 6–7 minutes. The cakes should be very soft to the touch. Turn out and serve immediately.

Tip: You can use silicone moulds but turning out will be a little more difficult.

Four variations on a white chocolate fondant

Make the basic fondant mixture (see page 16).

Half fill the greased and floured moulds with the mixture then place one of the following on top…

Totally chocolate *(top left)*
2 squares of white chocolate

Blueberry *(top right)*
1 teaspoon of blueberry jam

Nougat centre *(bottom left)*
1 cube of nougat (about 2 cm/¾ inch), softened and rolled into a ball

Chestnut *(bottom right)*
1 teaspoon of chestnut paste

…now fill the moulds two-thirds of the way up with the remaining mixture and cook as on page 16.

Tip: You can prepare the bases for these fondants in advance and keep them in the freezer (in a silicone mould). This will make it easier and faster to experiment with different fillings.

Runny caramel fondants

Preparation time: 10 minutes
Cooking time: 7–8 minutes
Makes 4 fondants

150 g (5¼ oz) caster sugar
100 g (3½ oz) salted butter
6 dessertspoons whipping cream
4 eggs
140 g (5 oz) plain flour

Preheat the oven to 180°C (fan oven 160°C), Gas Mark 4.

Use four metal dessert moulds. Grease and dust with flour or line with baking parchment. Place them on a baking tray covered with greaseproof paper.

In a saucepan, make a caramel with the sugar and 1 dessertspoon of water. Cook until it is a good colour.

Add the butter and cream and set aside to cool.

Add the eggs and the sieved flour. Mix together.

Fill the moulds three-quarters full. Cook for 7–8 minutes. Turn out carefully and serve immediately.

Tip: Again, the length of time you cook the fondants for determines how runny the centres will be.

Pistachio fondants with marzipan centres

Preparation time: 20 minutes +
1 hour freezing
Cooking time: 10 minutes
Makes 4 fondants

Pistachio sponge
1 egg
1 egg yolk
100 g (3½ oz) icing sugar
100 g (3½ oz) unsalted pistachios,
ground to a powder
6 dessertspoons whipping cream
1 teaspoon pistachio paste
70 g (2½ oz) butter, melted

Marzipan centres
4 large cubes of marzipan
3 dessertspoons whipping cream

For the pistachio sponge, beat the egg and the egg yolk with the icing sugar. Add the ground pistachios and beat again. Add the cream, pistachio paste and butter, mix together then chill in the fridge.

For the marzipan centres, mix the marzipan and cream together. Form into balls with your hands then put them in the freezer for 1 hour.

Preheat the oven to 200°C (fan oven 180°C), Gas Mark 6.

Use four metal dessert moulds. Grease and dust with flour or line with baking parchment. Place them on a baking tray covered with greaseproof paper.

Fill the moulds two-thirds full with the pistachio sponge mixture. Place a marzipan ball in the centre of each mould. Cook for 10 minutes.

Tips: Pistachio goes really well with chocolate, so you could give these fondants chocolate-flavoured centres.

Pistachio paste is available online or from specialist food stores.

Chestnut fondants

Preparation time: 20 minutes +
30 minutes resting
Cooking time: 7–8 minutes
Makes 4 fondants

Chestnut sponge
2 eggs
60 g (2 oz) butter, melted
30 g (1 oz) plain flour
200 g (7 oz) chestnut paste
50 g (1¾ oz) candied chestnuts,
chopped

Chestnut centres
50 g (1¾ oz) chestnut paste
1 dessertspoon thick double cream

For the sponge, beat the eggs and add the melted butter, flour and chestnut paste. Mix in the candied chestnuts.

For the chestnut centres, mix the chestnut paste and the cream together.

Use four metal dessert moulds. Grease and dust with flour or line with baking parchment. Place them on a baking tray covered with greaseproof paper.

Fill the moulds three-quarters full with the sponge mixture and put them in the fridge for 30 minutes.

Preheat the oven to 180°C (fan oven 160°C), Gas Mark 4.

Remove the moulds from the fridge, add 1 teaspoon of chestnut cream to the centre of each and cook for 7–8 minutes. Turn out gently.

Tip: Serve with a dollop of whipped cream and perhaps some small pieces of meringue for added crunch… Yum!

Almond fondants

Preparation time: 20 minutes +
30 minutes resting
Cooking time: 7–8 minutes
Makes 4 fondants

Almond sponge

1 egg
1 egg yolk
100 g (3½ oz) icing sugar
100 g (3½ oz) ground almonds
6 dessertspoons whipping cream
70 g (2½ oz) butter, melted
a few drops of bitter almond
  essence

Almond centres

50 g (1¾ oz) almond paste
1 dessertspoon whipping cream
25 g (¾ oz) white chocolate, broken
  into small pieces

For the sponge, mix the eggs, sugar
and ground almonds together. Add
the cream and melted butter then the
almond essence. Mix again.

Divide the mixture between four
muffin moulds or paper cases then
put in the fridge for 30 minutes.

For the almond centres, mix the
almond paste and the cream
together. Melt the white chocolate in
a bowl over a pan of simmering water
(make sure the white chocolate does
not get too hot) then add the almond
cream. Mix together.

Preheat the oven to 180°C (fan oven
160°C), Gas Mark 4.

Remove the moulds from the fridge
and add a teaspoon of the almond
cream to the centre of each. Cook for
7–8 minutes.

Tip: Almonds and fruit work perfectly
together, so add a good teaspoon of
jam to the centre of the fondants and
voila, a delicious new cake!

Ganache centres

Makes enough for about 20 fondant centres

Dark chocolate ganache
200 g (7 oz) dark chocolate
70 g (2½ oz) butter
5 dessertspoons whipping cream

Milk chocolate ganache
200 g (7 oz) milk chocolate
50 g (1¾ oz) butter
4 dessertspoons whipping cream

White chocolate ganache
200 g (7 oz) white chocolate
50 g (1¾ oz) butter
2 dessertspoons whipping cream

Pistachio and chocolate ganache
200 g (7 oz) white chocolate
2 dessertspoons whipping cream
2 dessertspoons pistachio paste

Raspberry and chocolate ganache
200 g (7 oz) white chocolate
100 g (3½ oz) crushed raspberries
50 g (1¾ oz) raspberry coulis

Another way of getting melting middles is by making chocolate-based centres, or ganaches. They allow you to create many different combinations and can be prepared in advance. The technique for making them is the same for all types of chocolate (dark, white or milk).

Melt the chocolate in a bowl over a pan of simmering water with the butter, cream and any flavouring. Mix to get a really smooth paste. *(top right)*

Fill a hemispherical silicone mould tray (or an ice cube tray) with the ganache. Put in the fridge (or freezer depending on the recipe). *(bottom left)*

When cooking the fondants, pop the ganache centres out of their trays, make a ball out of two hemispheres and place them in the centre of the raw fondants. *(bottom right)*

Dark chocolate fondants with orange centres

Preparation time: 20 minutes +
1 hour chilling
Cooking time: 6–7 minutes
Makes 4 fondants

Orange ganache

60 g (2 oz) milk chocolate, broken
into small pieces
1 dessertspoon whipping cream
a dash of Cointreau
grated zest of 1 orange
10 g (¼ oz) candied orange peel

Dark chocolate sponge

2 eggs
50 g (1¾ oz) brown sugar
1 dessertspoon plain flour
1 dessertspoon cornflour
140 g (5 oz) dark chocolate
(minimum 70% cocoa solids),
broken into small pieces
110 g (4 oz) butter
3 dessertspoons whipping cream

To make the orange ganache, melt
the milk chocolate, cream and
Cointreau in a bowl over a pan of
simmering water. Add the orange zest
and candied peel and stir in.

Pour into hemispherical silicone
moulds and leave in the fridge for
1 hour.

While the ganache is cooling, make
the sponge. Beat the eggs and brown
sugar together until pale. Sieve the
flour and cornflour together, add to
the mixture and continue to beat.

Melt the chocolate, butter and cream
together in a bowl over a pan of
simmering water.

Add the melted chocolate to the
sponge mixture and stir until you have
a smooth paste. Leave to cool in the
fridge for an hour.

Preheat the oven to 200°C (fan oven
180°C), Gas Mark 6.

Use four metal dessert moulds.
Grease and dust with flour or line
with baking parchment. Place them
on a baking tray covered with
greaseproof paper.

Fill the moulds with the sponge
mixture. Put an orange centre (made
from two hemispheres) in the middle
of each, pressing in lightly. Cook for
6–7 minutes.

Tip: You can decorate each fondant
with a little candied peel if you like.

Milk chocolate fondants with caramel centres

Preparation time: 20 minutes +
1 hour freezing
Cooking time: 6–7 minutes
Makes 4 fondants

Carambar ganache
2 Carambar caramels (or 20 g/¾ oz
chewy toffees)
2 dessertspoons whipping cream
50 g (1¾ oz) milk chocolate, broken
into small pieces

Milk chocolate sponge
3 eggs
80 g (2¾ oz) caster sugar
1 dessertspoon plain flour
150 g (5¼ oz) milk chocolate,
broken into small pieces
40 g (1½ oz) butter

For the Carambar ganache, melt the Carambars and cream in a bowl over a pan of simmering water then add the chocolate. Stir until melted.

Pour into hemispherical silicone moulds and put in the freezer for 1 hour.

Meanwhile, prepare the sponge. Mix the eggs and sugar together and beat until pale. Add the sieved flour and continue to beat. Melt the milk chocolate and butter in a bowl over a pan of simmering water.

Pour the melted chocolate into the sponge mixture and mix until you have a smooth paste.

Preheat the oven to 200°C (fan oven 180°C), Gas Mark 6.

Use four individual dessert moulds. Grease and dust with flour or line with baking parchment. Place them on a baking tray covered with greaseproof paper.

Fill the moulds with the sponge mixture. Add a Carambar centre (made from two hemispheres) to the middle of each and press in lightly. Cook for 6–7 minutes.

Tip: Carambar is a long chewy caramel sweet from France.

Dark chocolate fondants with vanilla centres

Preparation time: 20 minutes +
1 hour freezing
Cooking time: 6–7 minutes
Makes 4 fondants

Vanilla centres

1 egg
2 dessertspoons caster sugar
1 dessertspoon plain flour
100 ml (3½ fl oz) milk
10 g (¼ oz) butter
1 vanilla pod
2 dessertspoons whipping cream

Dark chocolate sponge

2 eggs
50 g (1¾ oz) brown sugar
1 dessertspoon plain flour
1 dessertspoon cornflour
140 g (5 oz) dark chocolate
  (minimum 70% cocoa solids),
  broken into small pieces
110 g (4 oz) butter
3 dessertspoons whipping cream

For the vanilla centres, beat the egg and sugar together until the mixture pales. Add the sieved flour and beat.

Boil the milk with the butter and scraped vanilla pod. Pour over the beaten egg mixture, mix, return to the saucepan and cook over a low heat for 10 minutes, stirring often until the cream thickens. Throw away the vanilla pod.

Leave the vanilla cream to cool. When it is tepid, whisk the very cold cream until firm. Mix into the vanilla cream with a spatula.

Freeze for 1 hour in hemispherical silicone moulds.

Meanwhile, prepare the sponge mix. Beat the eggs and brown sugar together until pale. Sieve the flour and cornflour together, add to the mixture and continue to beat. Melt the chocolate, butter and cream in a bowl over a pan of simmering water. Add to the sponge mixture and mix until you have a smooth paste. Leave to cool in the fridge for 1 hour.

Preheat the oven to 200°C (fan oven 180°C), Gas Mark 6.

Grease and flour four silicone moulds and fill with the sponge mixture. Put a vanilla centre (made from two hemispheres) in the centre of each, pressing in gently. Cook for 6–7 minutes.

Dark chocolate fondants with coffee centres

Preparation time: 20 minutes +
 1 hour freezing
Cooking time: 6–7 minutes
Makes 4 fondants

Coffee ganache
50 g (1¾ oz) dark chocolate, broken
 into small pieces
1 dessertspoon whipping cream
½ an espresso coffee

Dark chocolate sponge
2 eggs
50 g (1¾ oz) brown sugar
1 dessertspoon plain flour
1 dessertspoon cornflour
140 g (5 oz) dark chocolate
 (minimum 70% cocoa solids),
 broken into small pieces
110 g (4 oz) butter
3 dessertspoons whipping cream

To make the coffee ganache, melt the chocolate, cream and coffee in a bowl over a pan of simmering water.

Pour into hemispherical silicone moulds and leave in the freezer for 1 hour.

Meanwhile, prepare the sponge. Beat the eggs and brown sugar together until pale. Sieve the flour and cornflour together, add to the mixture and continue to beat.

Melt the chocolate, butter and cream together in a bowl over a pan of simmering water.

Mix the melted chocolate with the sponge mixture until you have a smooth paste.

Preheat the oven to 200°C (fan oven 180°C), Gas Mark 6.

Use four metal dessert moulds. Grease and dust with flour or line with baking parchment. Place them on a baking tray covered with greaseproof paper.

Fill the moulds with the sponge mixture. Put a coffee centre (made from two hemispheres) in the middle of each cake, pressing in gently. Cook for 6–7 minutes.

Dark chocolate fondants with raspberry centres

Preparation time: 20 minutes +
  1 hour freezing
Cooking time: 7–8 minutes
Makes 4 fondants

Raspberry ganache
30 g (1 oz) white chocolate, broken
  into small pieces
2 dessertspoons whipping cream
30 g (1 oz) raspberry coulis
10 g (¼ oz) fresh raspberries,
  roughly chopped

Dark chocolate sponge
2 eggs
50 g (1¾ oz) brown sugar
1 dessertspoon plain flour
1 dessertspoon cornflour
140 g (5 oz) dark chocolate
  (minimum 70% cocoa solids),
  broken into small pieces
110 g (4 oz) butter
3 dessertspoons whipping cream

For the raspberry ganache, melt the white chocolate in a bowl over a pan of simmering water (make sure the white chocolate does not get too hot) then add the cream, raspberry coulis and fresh raspberries. Pour into hemispherical silicone moulds and freeze for 1 hour.

Meanwhile, prepare the sponge. Beat the eggs and brown sugar together until pale. Sieve the flour and cornflour together, add to the mixture and continue to beat. Melt the chocolate, butter and cream in a bowl over a pan of simmering water.

Mix the melted chocolate with the sponge mixture until you have a smooth paste.

Preheat the oven to 200°C (fan oven 180°C), Gas Mark 6.

Use four metal dessert moulds. Grease and dust with flour or line with baking parchment. Place them on a baking tray covered with greaseproof paper.

Fill the moulds with the sponge mixture. Put a raspberry centre (made from two hemispheres) in the middle of each cake, pressing in gently. Cook for 7–8 minutes.

Tip: The fresh raspberries really make these fondants: they add a slight touch of acidity for a perfect equilibrium.

Raspberry fondants with dark chocolate centres

Preparation time: 10 minutes +
1 hour freezing
Cooking time: 6–7 minutes
Makes 4 fondants

Dark chocolate ganache
70 g (2½ oz) dark chocolate, broken
into small pieces
20 g (¾ oz) butter
3 dessertspoons whipping cream

Raspberry sponge
3 eggs
80 g (2¾ oz) caster sugar
2 heaped dessertspoons cornflour
200 g (7 oz) raspberry coulis
50 g (1¾ oz) fresh raspberries,
roughly chopped

To make the dark chocolate ganache, melt the chocolate, butter and cream in a bowl over a pan of simmering water. Pour into hemispherical silicone moulds and freeze for 1 hour.

Meanwhile, prepare the sponge. Beat the eggs and sugar together until pale. Add the cornflour, raspberry coulis and finally the raspberries.

Preheat the oven to 200°C (fan oven 180°C), Gas Mark 6.

Grease and flour four individual moulds. Fill two-thirds full with the sponge mixture. Put a dark chocolate middle (made from two hemispheres) in the centre of each, pressing in gently. Cook for 6–7 minutes. Turn out carefully.

Tip: A little lightly sweetened mascarpone, a pinch of cinnamon or some coriander seeds will all enhance this combination of chocolate and raspberries.

Chocolate and vanilla fondants with milk chocolate centres

Preparation time: 20 minutes +
  1 hour chilling
Cooking time: 10 minutes
Makes 4 fondants

Chocolate and vanilla sponge
110 g (4 oz) plain flour
2 eggs
90 g (3¼ oz) caster sugar
125 g (4½ oz) butter, melted
1 vanilla pod
100 ml (3½ fl oz) whipping cream
40 g (1½ oz) cocoa powder

Milk chocolate ganache
100 g (3½ oz) milk chocolate,
  broken into small pieces
2 dessertspoons whipping cream
50 g (1¾ oz) butter

For the sponge, sieve the flour, add the eggs one by one then the sugar and the melted butter. Mix until you have a smooth paste.

Divide the paste in half. Scrape the seeds from the vanilla pod into one half of the mixture.

Heat the cream and melt the cocoa powder in the hot cream. Add this to the other half of the mixture.

Pour a bit of each of the two mixtures into four hemispherical silicone moulds, making sure they overlap each other, then place in the fridge for 1 hour.

To make the milk chocolate ganache, melt the chocolate, cream and butter in a bowl over a pan of simmering water. Pour into hemispherical silicone moulds and leave to freeze for 1 hour.

Preheat the oven to 200°C (fan oven 180°C), Gas Mark 6.

Remove the fondants from the fridge and add a milk chocolate centre (made from two hemispheres) to each, pressing lightly. Cook for 10 minutes.

Dark chocolate fondants with pistachio centres

Preparation time: 20 minutes +
  1 hour freezing
Cooking time: 6–7 minutes
Makes 4 fondants

Pistachio ganache
100 g (3½ oz) white chocolate,
  broken into small pieces
1 dessertspoon pistachio paste
10 g (¼ oz) pistachio nuts, crushed
3 dessertspoons whipping cream

Dark chocolate sponge
2 eggs
50 g (1¾ oz) brown sugar
1 dessertspoon plain flour
1 dessertspoon cornflour
140 g (5 oz) dark chocolate
  (minimum 70% cocoa solids),
  broken into small pieces
110 g (4 oz) butter
3 dessertspoons whipping cream

For the pistachio ganache, melt the white chocolate with the pistachio paste, crushed pistachios and cream in a bowl over a pan of simmering water (make sure the white chocolate does not get too hot). Pour into hemispherical silicone moulds and freeze for 1 hour.

Meanwhile, prepare the sponge. Beat the eggs and brown sugar together until pale. Sieve the flour and cornflour together, add to the mixture and continue to beat. Melt the chocolate, butter and cream in a bowl over a pan of simmering water.

Mix the melted chocolate with the sponge mixture until you have a smooth paste.

Preheat the oven to 200°C (fan oven 180°C), Gas Mark 6.

Use four metal dessert moulds. Grease and dust with flour or line with baking parchment. Place them on a baking tray covered with greaseproof paper.

Fill the moulds with the sponge mixture. Add a pistachio centre (made from two hemispheres) to each and press lightly. Cook for 6–7 minutes.

Tip: You can find pistachio paste in specialist shops or online, or you could make your own. It's best to choose a paste with no added colouring to avoid having a very brightly coloured fondant.

Mint chocolate fondants

Preparation time: 20 minutes +
1 hour freezing
Cooking time: 6–7 minutes
Makes 4 fondants

Vanilla and mint centres
1 egg
2 dessertspoons caster sugar
1 dessertspoon plain flour
100 ml (3½ fl oz) milk
10 g (¼ oz) butter
1 vanilla pod
7 dessertspoons whipping cream
6 fresh mint leaves, finely chopped

Dark chocolate sponge
2 eggs
50 g (1¾ oz) brown sugar
1 dessertspoon plain flour
1 dessertspoon cornflour
140 g (5 oz) dark chocolate
  (minimum 70% cocoa solids),
  broken into small pieces
110 g (4 oz) butter
3 dessertspoons whipping cream
1 dessertspoon white mint syrup

To make the vanilla and mint centres, beat the egg and sugar together until the mixture turns pale. Add the sieved flour and beat again.

Boil the milk, butter and scraped vanilla pod together. Pour over the egg mixture, mix and return to the saucepan to cook over a low heat for 10 minutes, stirring constantly until the mixture thickens. Remove the vanilla pod.

Leave the vanilla cream to cool. When it is lukewarm, whisk the very cold cream until it is stiff. Add to the vanilla cream with the chopped mint, folding in with a spatula.

Pour into hemispherical silicone moulds and freeze for 1 hour.

Meanwhile, prepare the sponge. Beat the eggs and brown sugar together until pale. Sieve the flour and cornflour together, add to the mixture and continue to beat.

Melt the chocolate, butter and cream in a bowl over a pan of simmering water.

Add the melted chocolate to the sponge mixture and mix together until you have a smooth paste. Add the mint syrup.

Preheat the oven to 200°C (fan oven 180°C), Gas Mark 6.

Grease and flour four individual moulds and fill with the sponge mixture. Add a vanilla and mint centre (made from two hemispheres) to each and press lightly. Cook for 6–7 minutes.

Chestnut fondants with hazelnut centres

Preparation time: 20 minutes +
  1 hour freezing
Cooking time: 7–8 minutes
Makes 4 fondants

Hazelnut centres
50 g (1¾ oz) pralinoise chocolate or
  milk chocolate with hazelnuts
10 g (¼ oz) salted butter
2 dessertspoons whipping cream
2 dessertspoons ground hazelnuts

Chestnut sponge
2 eggs
60 g (2 oz) butter, melted
30 g (1 oz) plain flour
200 g (7 oz) chestnut paste
50 g (1¾ oz) candied chestnuts,
  chopped

To make the hazelnut centres, melt the pralinoise, butter and cream in a bowl over a pan of simmering water. Add the ground hazelnuts. Pour into an ice cube tray and freeze for 1 hour.

Meanwhile, prepare the sponge. Beat the eggs, add the melted butter, flour, chestnut paste and candied chestnuts and mix well.

Use four metal dessert moulds. Grease and dust with flour or line with baking parchment. Place them on a baking tray covered with greaseproof paper. Fill the moulds three-quarters full with the sponge mixture and set aside in the fridge for 30 minutes.

Preheat the oven to 180°C (fan oven 160°C), Gas Mark 4. Remove the fondants from the fridge and add a hazelnut centre to each. Cook for 7–8 minutes. Turn out carefully.

Tip: To make turning these cakes out really easy, use stainless steel baking rings, lined with greaseproof paper.

Hazelnut fondants with ginger centres

Preparation time: 20 minutes +
1 hour freezing
Cooking time: 7–8 minutes
Makes 4 fondants

Hazelnut sponge

1 egg
1 egg yolk
100 g (3½ oz) icing sugar
80 g (2¾ oz) ground hazelnuts
5 ginger biscuits, crushed to a
powder
6 dessertspoons whipping cream
70 g (2½ oz) butter, melted
50 g (1¾ oz) hazelnuts, roughly
chopped

Ginger ganache

50 g (1¾ oz) milk chocolate, broken
into small pieces
2 dessertspoons whipping cream
15 g (½ oz) salted butter
1 ginger biscuit, crushed

Prepare the sponge. Mix together the eggs, icing sugar, ground hazelnuts and ginger biscuits. Add the cream and melted butter then the chopped hazelnuts. Mix well and set aside in the fridge.

To make the ganache, melt the milk chocolate, cream and butter in a bowl over a pan of simmering water. Add the ginger biscuit. Pour into hemispherical silicone moulds and freeze for 1 hour.

Preheat the oven to 180°C (fan oven 160°C), Gas Mark 4.

Use four metal dessert moulds. Grease and dust with flour or line with baking parchment. Place them on a baking tray covered with greaseproof paper.

Fill the moulds two-thirds full with the sponge mixture. Add a ginger centre (made from two hemispheres) to each and press lightly. Cook for 7–8 minutes.

Orange fondants with Grand Marnier centres

Preparation time: 20 minutes +
1 hour freezing
Cooking time: 15 minutes
Makes 6 fondants

Grand Marnier ganache
75 g (2½ oz) white chocolate,
broken into small pieces
50 ml (1¾ fl oz) Grand Marnier

Orange sponge
2 eggs
125 g (4½ oz) caster sugar
75 g (2½ oz) plain flour
½ sachet yeast
50 g (1¾ oz) semolina
125 g (4½ oz) butter, melted
zest and juice of half an orange

Syrup
zest and juice of 1 orange
50 g (1¾ oz) brown sugar
50 ml (1¾ fl oz) Grand Marnier

To make the ganache, melt the white chocolate and Grand Marnier in a bowl over a pan of simmering water (make sure the white chocolate does not get too hot). Stir. Pour into hemispherical silicone moulds and freeze for 1 hour.

Meanwhile, prepare the sponge. Beat the eggs and sugar together until they turn pale.

Mix the flour, yeast and semolina together and add to the eggs and sugar with the melted butter. Add the orange zest and juice then place in the fridge.

To make the syrup, mix the orange zest and juice with the sugar and Grand Marnier and boil for 5 minutes.

Preheat the oven to 180°C (fan oven 160°C), Gas Mark 4.

Grease and flour six individual moulds, place a paper case in each and fill two-thirds full with the sponge mixture. Add a Grand Marnier centre (made from two hemispheres) to each and press lightly. Cook for around 15 minutes.

Heat the orange syrup on removing the cakes from the oven. Turn the fondants out once they have cooled and serve with the syrup.

Tips: Decorate with extra orange peel, if you wish.

You can vary this citrus and liqueur combination by trying any number of ingredients. For example, try grapefruit and amaretto or lemon and limoncello.

Ginger fondants with mango centres

Preparation time: 10 minutes +
   1 hour freezing
Cooking time: 10 minutes
Makes 4 fondants

Ginger sponge
110 g (4 oz) plain flour
½ sachet yeast
2 eggs
100 g (3½ oz) butter, melted
110 g (4 oz) caster sugar
30 g (1 oz) fresh ginger, peeled and
   grated

Mango ganache
50 g (1¾ oz) fresh mango, puréed
1 teaspoon honey
50 g (1¾ oz) white chocolate,
   broken into small pieces

For the sponge, mix the flour and yeast together, add the eggs then the melted butter and sugar. Add the grated ginger and mix together. Set aside in the fridge.

To make the mango ganache, mix the mango and honey together. Melt the white chocolate in a bowl over a pan of simmering water (make sure the white chocolate does not get too hot) then add the mango mixture. Pour into hemispherical silicone moulds and freeze for 1 hour.

Preheat the oven to 180°C (fan oven 160°C), Gas Mark 4.

Use four metal dessert moulds. Grease and dust with flour or line with baking parchment. Place them on a baking tray covered with greaseproof paper.

Fill two-thirds full with the sponge mixture. Add a mango centre (made from two hemispheres) to each, pressing lightly. Cook for 10 minutes. Allow to cool before turning out.

Quick fruit centres

Preparation time: 10 minutes
Cooking time: 45 minutes

500 g (1 lb 1½ oz) fruit
500 g (1 lb 1½ oz) caster sugar +
  extra for dusting

Teatime is a time for kids, a time for them to enjoy making these fruity cubes that will soon fill their favourite cakes. This recipe works for fruits such as raspberries, strawberries, quinces, plums, apricots…

Cook the fruit and sugar in a heavy-based saucepan, stirring constantly until the mixture comes away from the bottom of the pan; you should be able to see the bottom of the pan for 3–4 seconds after passing a spoon through (this will take around 45 minutes).

Pour the mixture into a silicone mould or a mould that has been lined with greaseproof paper. Leave to dry then turn out, cut into cubes and roll in caster sugar.

When cooking the cakes, place the cubes of fruit on the cake mixture and cover with a little more mixture. Keep the remaining cubes in an airtight container.

If you don't feel confident making your own fruit pastes, you could use your favourite jam as a filling.

Top left – choose well-ripened seasonal fruit.

Top right – you must stir constantly so that the mixture does not stick to the bottom of the pan.

Bottom left – ice cube trays make very handy portions of fruit fillings.

Bottom right – do not fill the cake moulds to the top as you will be in danger of the mixture overflowing.

Mini cake fondants with fruit centres

Preparation time: 10 minutes
Cooking time: 10 minutes
Makes 6 cakes

fruit centres of your choice (see page 56)

Cake
2 eggs
50 g (1¾ oz) caster sugar
150 g (5¼ oz) plain flour
½ sachet yeast
90 g (3¼ oz) butter, melted
4 dessertspoons whipping cream

Beat the eggs and sugar together. Add the flour and yeast, followed by the butter and cream. Mix well until you have a runny paste.

Preheat the oven to 180°C (fan oven 160°C), Gas Mark 4.

Fill individual silicone mini cake moulds two-thirds full with the cake mixture. Put a fruit centre (see previous page) into each and press in lightly. Cook for 10 minutes.

Tips: As well as using fruit centres, you can embellish the cake mixture a little if you like.

Blackberry centre *(top left)*
Use a blackberry centre and add the zest and the juice of 1 lime to the cake mix.

Raspberry centre *(bottom left)*
Use a raspberry centre and add 50 g (1¾ oz) of fresh raspberries to the cake mix.

Strawberry centre *(top right)*
Use a strawberry centre and add seeds from a vanilla pod to the cake mix.

Apricot centre *(bottom right)*
Use an apricot centre and add strips of fresh apricot to the cake mix.

Coconut fondants with exotic fruit centres

Preparation time: 20 minutes +
2 hours freezing
Cooking time: 10 minutes
Makes 6 fondants

Exotic fruit centres
50 g (1¾ oz) caster sugar
100 g (3½ oz) fruit (e.g. mango,
 pineapple), peeled and puréed
50 ml (1¾ fl oz) dark rum

Coconut sponge
2 eggs
100 g (3½ oz) caster sugar
180 g (6¼ oz) dessicated coconut

For the fruit centres, melt the sugar in a little water and heat until it turns pale gold. Add the fruit purée, pour in the rum and flambé. Leave to reduce until the mixture becomes jam-like.

Pour the fruit into small silicone moulds and freeze for 2 hours.

Meanwhile, prepare the coconut sponge. Beat the eggs and sugar until the mixture becomes pale. Add the coconut and beat again.

Preheat the oven to 180°C (fan oven 160°C), Gas Mark 4.

Fill six moulds two-thirds full with the sponge mixture, add a fruit centre to each then cover with more sponge mixture. Cook for 10 minutes.

Cherry clafoutis fondants

Preparation time: 1 hour + 1 hour
  freezing
Cooking time: 10 minutes
Makes 6 mini clafoutis

50 g (1¾ oz) caster sugar, for
  dusting

Clafoutis batter
2 eggs
100 g (3½ oz) plain flour
150 g (5¼ oz) milk
100 ml (3½ fl oz) whipping cream

Cherry centres
100 g (3½ oz) ripe cherries, stoned
75 g (2½ oz) caster sugar
50 ml (1¾ fl oz) kirsch

For the clafoutis, mix the eggs into the flour one by one, being careful not to make any lumps. Add the milk and the cream until you have a very runny batter.

Divide one-third of the mixture between six cake moulds then put them in the freezer for 1 hour. Leave the rest of the mix in the fridge.

To make the cherry centres, cook the cherries, sugar and kirsch over a low heat for 1 hour until they have formed a compote. Leave to cool.

Preheat the oven to 200°C (fan oven 180°C), Gas Mark 6.

Take the moulds out of the freezer. Put 1 teaspoon of cherry compote in the centre of each mould then cover with more clafoutis mixture. Cook for 10 minutes then turn out gently. Sprinkle immediately with the sugar.

Tip: The basic mix is for a clafoutis; the idea is to find the fruity surprise when you plunge your spoon into the cake. Again, don't hesitate to experiment with different fruits and different flavours.

Pear muffins with fig centres

Preparation time: 10 minutes +
30 minutes resting
Cooking time: 10 minutes
Makes 6 muffins

Muffin mixture
2 pears, peeled
juice of 1 lemon
200 g (7 oz) plain flour
½ sachet yeast
150 g (5¼ oz) caster sugar
2 eggs
30 g (1 oz) butter, melted
100 ml (3½ fl oz) whipping cream

Fig centres
3 dried figs, finely chopped
1 fresh fig, finely chopped
50 ml (1¾ fl oz) Armagnac
50 g (1¾ oz) icing sugar

Cut one pear into small pieces and purée the other with the lemon juice.

Mix the flour, yeast and sugar together then add the eggs one by one with the melted butter and cream. Finally add the pears. Leave in the fridge for 30 minutes.

Mix all the ingredients for the fig centres together.

Preheat the oven to 180°C (fan oven 160°C), Gas Mark 4.

Fill six paper cases or muffin moulds with the sponge mixture, adding a good teaspoon of fig filling to the centre of each. Cook for 10 minutes.

Lemon tart muffins

Preparation time: 20 minutes +
1 hour freezing
Cooking time: 10 minutes
Makes 6 muffins

Muffin mixture
200 g (7 oz) plain flour
½ sachet yeast
150 g (5¼ oz) caster sugar
2 eggs
30 g (1 oz) butter, melted
100 ml (3½ fl oz) whipping cream
100 ml (3½ fl oz) limoncello
zest and juice of 2 lemons

Lemon centres
50 g (1¾ oz) butter
75 g (2½ oz) caster sugar
juice of 1 lemon
10 g (¼ oz) cornflour
1 egg

Combine the flour, yeast and sugar
then add the eggs one by one. Add
the butter, cream and limoncello then
the lemon zest and juice. Mix well
and set aside in the fridge.

For the lemon centres, melt the
butter, sugar and lemon juice
together. Add the cornflour and
egg and mix until you have a
smooth paste.

Pour into hemispherical silicone
moulds and freeze for 1 hour.

Preheat the oven to 180°C (fan oven
160°C), Gas Mark 4.

Fill six muffin moulds with the muffin
mixture and add a lemon centre
(made from two hemispheres) to
each. Cook for 10 minutes.

Custard (crème anglaise)

Preparation time: 5 minutes
Cooking time: 10 minutes

Basic recipe
8 egg yolks
200 g (7 oz) caster sugar
1 litre (1¾ pints) milk

Whisk the egg yolks with the sugar until the mixture turns pale.

Boil the milk, pour over the eggs and whisk.

Pour the mixture into another saucepan and cook over a low heat for 10 minutes, stirring constantly (be careful as the temperature should not go over 85°C/185°F). The custard is ready when it sticks to the back of a wooden spoon.

Tip: Try one of the following flavourings or experiment with your own:

Coffee *(top left)*
Add 2 espresso coffees to the cold milk and sprinkle with crushed coffee beans.

Pistachio *(bottom left)*
Add 1 dessertspoon of pistachio paste to the cold milk and sprinkle with chopped pistachio nuts.

Chocolate *(top right)*
Add 3 dessertspoons of cocoa powder to the cold milk.

Vanilla *(bottom right)*
Add a split, scraped vanilla pod to the cold milk.

Flavoured whipped creams and coulis

Creams

Plain
Mix 500 ml (17½ fl oz) of whipping cream with 150 g (5¼ oz) of icing sugar. Pour into a siphon and leave to cool.

Caramel
Heat 500 ml (17½ fl oz) of whipping cream and 10 Carambar caramels or 100 g (3½ oz) of chewy caramels. Pour into a siphon and leave to cool.

Fruit
Mix 500 ml (17½ fl oz) of whipping cream with 200 g (7 oz) of sieved fruit purée. Pour into a siphon and leave to cool.

Nutella
Heat 500 ml (17½ fl oz) of whipping cream and 150 g (5¼ oz) of Nutella. Pour into a siphon and leave to cool.

Liquorice
Heat 500 ml (17½ fl oz) of whipping cream and 4 sticks of liquorice. Add 100 g (3½ oz) of caster sugar. Pour into a siphon and leave to cool.

Syrup
Mix 500 ml (17½ fl oz) of whipping cream with 100 ml (3½ fl oz) of syrup (e.g. mint, barley, grenadine). Pour into a siphon and leave to cool.

Fruit coulis

Apricot
Cook 500 g (1 lb 1½ oz) of apricots, 150 g (5¼ oz) of icing sugar and 1 small bunch of lemon thyme for 20 minutes. Purée and serve cold.

Strawberry
Mix together 300 g (10½ oz) of fresh strawberries, the juice of 1 lemon, 6 basil leaves and 50 g (1¾ oz) of icing sugar. Sieve.

Blueberry
Mix together 300 g (10½ oz) of blueberries, 50 g (1¾ oz) of icing sugar and 100 ml (3½ fl oz) of sweet fortified wine. Sieve.

Peach
Plunge 500 g (1 lb 1½ oz) of peaches into a large pan of boiling water, peel and mix the flesh with 100 g (3½ oz) of caster sugar and a bunch of mint leaves. Purée.

Index

Conversion tables

The tables below are only approximate and are meant to be used as a guide only.

Approximate American/ European conversions

	USA	Metric	Imperial
brown sugar	1 cup	170 g	6 oz
butter	1 stick	115 g	4 oz
butter/ margarine/ lard	1 cup	225 g	8 oz
caster and granulated sugar	2 level tablespoons	30 g	1 oz
caster and granulated sugar	1 cup	225 g	8 oz
currants	1 cup	140 g	5 oz
flour	1 cup	140 g	5 oz
golden syrup	1 cup	350 g	12 oz
ground almonds	1 cup	115 g	4 oz
sultanas/ raisins	1 cup	200 g	7 oz

Approximate American/ European conversions

American	European
1 teaspoon	1 teaspoon/ 5 ml
½ fl oz	1 tablespoon/ ½ fl oz/ 15 ml
¼ cup	4 tablespoons/ 2 fl oz/ 50 ml
½ cup plus 2 tablespoons	¼ pint/ 5 fl oz/ 150 ml
1¼ cups	½ pint/ 10 fl oz/ 300 ml
1 pint/ 16 fl oz	1 pint/ 20 fl oz/ 600 ml
2½ pints (5 cups)	1.2 litres/ 2 pints
10 pints	4.5 litres/ 8 pints

Liquid measures

Imperial	ml	fl oz
1 teaspoon	5	
2 tablespoons	30	
4 tablespoons	60	
¼ pint/ 1 gill	150	5
⅓ pint	200	7
½ pint	300	10
¾ pint	425	15
1 pint	600	20
1¾ pints	1000 (1 litre)	35

Oven temperatures

American	Celsius	Fahrenheit	Gas Mark
Cool	130	250	½
Very slow	140	275	1
Slow	150	300	2
Moderate	160	320	3
Moderate	180	350	4
Moderately hot	190	375	5
Fairly hot	200	400	6
Hot	220	425	7
Very hot	230	450	8
Extremely hot	240	475	9

Other useful measurements

Measurement	Metric	Imperial
1 American cup	225 ml	8 fl oz
1 egg, size 3	50 ml	2 fl oz
1 egg white	30 ml	1 fl oz
1 rounded tablespoon flour	30 g	1 oz
1 rounded tablespoon cornflour	30 g	1 oz
1 rounded tablespoon caster sugar	30 g	1 oz
2 level teaspoons gelatine	10 g	¼ oz